ADVERSITY, TRIALS, AND TRIBULATIONS

THE FIRE OF GOD

TERRY L. SCOTT

Copyright © 2021 Terry L. Scott
All rights reserved. No part of this book may be used or reproduced by any means, graphic, electronic, or mechanical, including photocopying, recording, taping, or by any information storage retrieval system without the written permission of the publisher except in the case of brief quotations embodied in critical articles and reviews.

Scriptures are taken from the English Standard and the King James Version of the Bible.

RSIP
Raising the Standard International Publishing LLC books may be ordered by contacting
rsim.terryscott@gmail.com
Culpeper, Virginia

ISBN: 978-1-955830-40-9
Printed in the United States of America
1st Edition December 2021

DEDICATION

This book is dedicated to the Lord Jesus Christ, who has given me new life through the death, burial, and resurrection by the cross, allowing me to walk in the newness of life, with Him beside me all the time.

The Holy Spirit has taught me to walk each day, one day at a time. Doing so has helped me see the physical issues around my life and understand daily spiritual ones. How will I fight and win them while still being able to discern what the Lord is saying?

I will not forget to name my wife, Ana, by allowing me the freedom to write and to truly show me the Proverbs 31 woman He gave to me.

TABLE OF CONTENTS

1	Introduction	1
2	A Generation Of God-Seekers	5
3	The Sons Of Levi	10
4	The Importance Of The Old Testament Scriptures	18
5	The Old Testament Levi Is The New Testament Believer	25
6	How Are Gold And Silver Refined?	34
7	A Heart That Is Refined	37
8	A Heart That Has Alloys Added	41
9	Our Lord Jesus Christ Is Returning For Believers With A Refined Heart	43
10	Removing The Alloys That Cause Corrosion	46
11	God Will Use His To Fire To Refine Us	53
12	God Uses Adversity, Trials, And Tribulations As A Means Of His Refining Fire	57
13	The Wilderness Experience	64
14	The Wilderness Experience Would Seem As Though God Has Forsaken Us	69
15	The Wilderness Experience May	71

	Spark The Question, "Where Is Your God?"	
16	Understanding The Times That We Are In	75
17	God Desires To Reveal What He Is Doing And Why He Is Doing What He Is Doing	79
18	Typical Responses From Believers To Trials, Tribulations, And The Wilderness Times	84
19	Why Do We Go Through The Tough Times?	89
20	The Trials Of My Life	100
	Conclusion	115
	About The Author	117

ACKNOWLEDGEMENTS

I would like to thank the Lord Jesus Christ, who has been with me writing this book. The Lord has sent many people in my life during a trying and difficult time to help ease the pain of suffering I have had to endure. They showed me the encouragement and strength in many situations to overcome the evil one when I felt weak and destroyed.

I owe everything to Jesus because He is the one who created me and knew me in my mother's womb before I was born. Yet He chose to suffer for me on a Cross for all the pain I would ever have to go through. He brought me Peace (Shalom) during the storms of my life. And I know He will continue to do so until the day he calls me back home, where I will forever be with the Lord. AMEN!!!

FOREWORD

"Adversity, Trials, and Tribulations" is more than just one man's battle with pain, suffering, sickness, and doubts. It is a book dealing with issues to which we all can relate. Every believer will face the "hard times." It is through our testing times that our life faces the crisis of faith. Just like we need to exercise our muscles for growth and strength, we need to do the same with our faith.

We all struggle at different times in life. Often it seems like each event is the straw that will break the camel's back. We become overwhelmed, seem defeated, and are wits in. The adversities, trials, and tribulations have come to the place that we have cried out to God many times, just like the apostle Paul. However, either God does not answer, or He responds with, "My grace is sufficient."

Terry addresses those times when faith and doubt meet head-on, and everything in our five senses tells us we are going underwater just like the Apostle Peter. However, just when we think God is playing hide and seek with us, He reaches out His hands and pulls us out of what seemingly appears to be a hopeless situation.

Are you in what seems to be a hopeless circumstance? Does it feel as though God has forsaken you? Have you tried everything "humanly" possible to crawl out of the hole of darkness you have found yourself? Maybe this book revealing Terry Scott's face with death might stir in you the faith needed to stand firm in the promises of our great God.

Terry dedicates this book to all who have gone through the fire, are currently in the fire, or will soon face the fire of adversity, trial, or tribulation.

Charles Morris
CEO RSIM/RSIP

CHAPTER 1

THE INTRODUCTION

When we pray and fast, we prepare ourselves for what the Lord is doing in this age and what He will do in our future. He is building a Temple for His presence.

> *Ephesians 2:21-22 (KJVA)*
> *21.In whom all the building fitly framed together groweth unto a holy temple in the Lord: 22. In whom ye also are builded together for a habitation of God through the Spirit.*

Growth in the Lord will not come through feel-good experiences. I love experiencing the presence of God through the anointing of the Holy Spirit, but that is not where I grow up in the Lord. Unfortunately, some believers are satisfied moving from one anointing service to another anointing service. It is not that God is against us having these times of refreshing while enjoying His manifested presence. It is just that we also need to embrace the trials and tribulations that come our way.

There is a maturity process that can happen in trials and tribulations. I might also note that this is not the only way a believer matures, but trials and testing are processes that all believers will go through. This maturity comes in how we respond to the trials and tribulations of life. This book covers the Fire of the Holy Spirit. The fire is not pleasant at the time. If we respond to the trials and tribulations in a proactive matter, then the purposes and plans of God are realized within us. Remember that John the Baptist said that the Lord Jesus Christ would baptize us with the Holy Spirit and with fire.

> ***Matthew 3:11 (KJVA)***
> *I indeed baptize you with water unto repentance: but he that cometh after me is mightier than I, whose shoes I am not worthy to bear: he shall baptize you with the Holy Ghost, and with Fire:*

The Lord has raised His Army here on the earth. We are His people to go forth and take back the land the enemy has kept from the people of God for so long. It is not an easy task,

Adversity, Trials, and Tribulations

but the Lord does not call the equipped. He equips the called. The Holy Spirit will guide us in all Truth and Righteousness. May the fire of God fall on all of us to make us and keep us in the coming days of evil upon the earth until the Lord Jesus Christ either calls us home or comes to take us to be with Him. EVEN SO COME LORD JESUS COME, (BO YESHUA BO).

Terry L. Scott

APPLICATION

List some of your past adversities, trials, and tribulations that you could see how the Father was using His refining fire to mold you.

CHAPTER 2

A GENERATION OF GOD-SEEKERS

We believe that God is raising a generation that will manifest His glory and not their own. It is a generation that chooses to allow God to complete the task of refining. This new generation of believers, better known as the remnant, will seek after God and the things of God. For years now, drug stores have been built throughout our cities to program society to take medication first and often. Medicine is essential and needed but should not be the first and immediate response in the life of a true believer.

We have come to a society where we hate any discomfort or pain and take medication at the first sign of either. How does this mentality affect a believer? The Lord instructs us to be a people of prayer and fasting. The Lord Jesus Christ is committed to presenting us as a pure, spotless people before the Father. The Fire of the Holy Spirit purges us of the things that hinder the process of holiness. Fasting and prayer help us see and identify the Father's areas to cleanse and buffet our flesh to become strong in the spirit-man.

> *Malachi 3:1-3 (KJVA)*
> *Behold, I will send my messenger, and he shall prepare the way before me: and the Lord, whom ye seek, shall suddenly come to His Temple, even the messenger of the covenant, whom ye delight in: behold, he shall come, saith the LORD of hosts. But who may abide the day of his coming? and who shall stand when he appeareth? for he is like a refiner's Fire, and like fullers' soap: And He shall sit as a refiner and purifier of silver: and he shall purify the sons of Levi, and purge them as gold and silver, that they may offer unto the LORD an offering in righteousness.*

> *2 Tim. 2:20-21 But in a great house there are not only vessels of gold and of silver, but also of wood and of earth; and some to honor, and some to dishonor. 21. If a man therefore purge himself from these, he shall be a vessel unto honor, sanctified, and meet for the master's use, and prepared unto every good work.*

Adversity, Trials, and Tribulations

Notice that there are two types of vessels within the Temple. There are vessels of honor, meaning that they are precious, and vessels of dishonor, meaning shameful and vile. To "purge" means "to cleanse thoroughly of impurities."

> **Jeremiah 15:19**
> **Therefore thus saith the LORD, If thou return, then will I bring thee again, and thou shalt stand before me: and if thou take forth the precious from the vile, thou shalt be as my mouth: let them return unto thee, but return not thou unto them.**

Jeremiah was before the Lord in chapter 15. You can see the dialogue between the Lord and Jeremiah. Hashem was tired of His people turning away from Him. The false prophets were speaking lies. They were claiming to be speaking from the Lord, yet they were talking from their own deceit. The Lord said in chapter 15 of Jeremiah that He had had it with them all and would destroy them. Jeremiah went on to speak and complained to Hashem (Lord). He pleads to the Lord to remember him. The Lord replied to Jeremiah that He would restore him to stand before the Lord. The Lord said He would revive Jeremiah if he spoke what is precious and not what is worthless. Jeremiah would speak for the Lord. The people would turn to Jeremiah, but he would not turn to them.

Hashem (Lord) is raising an army of believers who will do whatever it takes to spread the Gospel to the world before the great day of the Lord's return to the earth as the King of Kings and Lord of Lords in truth and righteousness. The Lord is calling all the believers together to lay aside the burdens that so easily set us back and would keep us from moving forward in Jesus. We can and must submit our whole lives before the Lord if we expect to see the power, authority, and hand of God move in our lives.

We are the Temple of God, and He will not dwell in an unrighteous vessel. That was why Jesus is calling us through the Holy Spirit to come to him, and he will show you who you are created to be as a Servant of the Lord.

Adversity, Trials, and Tribulations

APPLICATION

Knowing that the Father has called us to be vessels of honor, list the ways God has been working on you to separate you as His vessel of honor.

CHAPTER 3

THE SONS OF LEVI

Who are the "sons of Levi"?

Malachi 3:3 (NKJV)
And he shall sit as a refiner and purifier of silver: and he shall purify the sons of Levi, and purge them as gold and silver, that they may offer unto the LORD an offering in righteousness.

Exodus 6:16 These are the names of the sons of Levi according to their generations: Gershon, Kohath, and Merari, the years of the life of Levi being 137 years.

They were appointed as priests, and God chose them to serve in the tabernacle at the altar. Some were gatekeepers, some were musicians, and some took the tithes

The Lord elevated the tribe of Levi to perform holy service in the tabernacle of the desert and the Temple. It is an affirmative command for all Levites to be available and

Adversity, Trials, and Tribulations

prepared for Temple Service, as stated in the Torah, "The Levites shall be for Me" (Numbers 18:14), indicating the special relationship with the tribe of Levi is permanent. The prophet Jeremiah relates God's promise that there will always be Kohanim and Levites fit to serve: "As I will never renege on My covenant with day and night, so is my covenant with...the Levites, the Kohanim, My servants" (Jeremiah 33:21)

The choice of the tribe of Levi for the highest spiritual service was due to their ability to channel their strong character in the service of God. Levi, the son of Jacob, was chastised for his anger by his Father: "Cursed is their zealousness for it is brazen, and their wrath for it is hard. I will separate them in Ya'akov and scatter them throughout Israel" (Genesis 49:6-7).

Four generations later, Moses blessed the same tribe of Levi: "Your righteous men...keeper of Your Word and covenant; He shall teach Your judgment in Ya'akov and Your Torah in Israel...Blessed of God is his valor, and his actions are pleasing..." (Deuteronomy 33:8-11). The Levites were able to apply their physical and spiritual strength to fulfill God's will and gain the role of God's trusted servants forever.

The name Levi comes from the words "he shall accompany." The name Levi was given to the third son of Jacob and Leah to indicate that he was to bring a strengthening of the relationship between his parents; for now, with three children, Jacob would need to accompany his wife, Leah.

Therefore, it was a natural development that the task of the Levite was to accompany the Divine Presence and serve in the Temple. His role as teacher and spiritual example is to lead and accompany others back to their spiritual purpose. The Midrash relates that Levites will lead the people of Israel back to their Father in Heaven in the future.

Levi ben Ya'akov (Jacob), the Father of the tribe of Levites, lived 137 years, the longest of all of the sons of Jacob. He had a powerful influence on the spiritual development of his progeny and lived to see his great-grandsons, Moses and Aaron.

Adversity, Trials, and Tribulations

The tribe of Levi developed separately from the other tribes of Israel. During the period of the Egyptian bondage, the Levites avoided the slavery suffered by the others by maintaining their separateness in the land of Goshen, immersed in the tents of learning and maintaining the spiritual tradition of the Fathers.

The loyalty of the Levites was demonstrated at the example of the Golden Calf. The general population was influenced by the evil promptings of the mixed multitude. The Levites chose to support Moshe to avenge God's honor, rewarded with the spiritual service lost at that time by the firstborn of the other tribes. The Levites were tested and proved themselves able, thereby earning their elevated spiritual status.

The Levites were constantly willing to risk their lives for God's service. They carried the sanctified vessels of the tabernacle, which, if mishandled, resulted in death.

His role as Temple functionary balanced the independent nature of the Levite. The Levites carried the tabernacle and its vessels wanderings in the desert. Levites served as the honor guard, gatekeepers, and musicians of the Temple. They also assisted the Kohanim in preparing the offerings and in other aspects of the Temple's functioning.

The economics of the tribe of Levi were unique among the tribes of Israel. In contrast to the other tribes, Levites had no inherited portion in the Land of Israel. Forty-two cities scattered throughout the other tribes were set aside as cities of Levites. In these cities, the Levites served as spiritual teachers to the people of Israel. These cities also served as shelters for those guilty of accidentally causing a person's death. Whereas the other tribes worked the land, the Levite was dependent on the tithes and food gifts. Levites were to be economically dependent on others for their income. In exchange for his life's service, the Levite received God's ordained sustenance through the required tithing of the nation. There was a mitzvah upon the people of Israel not to abandon the tribe of Levi.

Levites were exempt from general military service and not counted in the census of the army in the time of Moses. Though

Adversity, Trials, and Tribulations

relieved of the specific mitzvah of waging war, they must take part in the mitzvah of saving lives in times of direct threat.

The service of the Levite is the service of the Spirit. Thus, the tribe originally chastised for its warlike behavior became the tribe which exemplified peace, blessing, and fraternal harmony. Yet the Levites throughout history were able to rise to the occasion to fight for values, when necessary, as in the case of Chanukah, where they led the Jewish struggle against Greek influence.

An exciting contrast to the general army exemption of the tribe of Levi was the office of the "Kohen Anointed for War." This Kohen, whose position was an honored one in the hierarchy of Kohanim, was appointed to inspire and spiritually prepare the army of Israel before the battle.

God's special relationship with the tribe of Levi promised to last forever. No other family is allowed to perform the Temple Service. Levites have been among the nation's spiritual leaders from the earliest times and continue to fulfill leadership roles until today.

The actual fulfillment of the soul of a son of the tribe of Levi is to serve God in the Holy Temple in Jerusalem once again.

APPLICATION

As God called and separated the Levitical priesthood to serve Him, He also called and separated us as the priesthood of believers to serve Him. In what ways are you serving the Father and the Lord Jesus Christ?

CHAPTER 4

THE IMPORTANCE OF THE OLD TESTAMENT SCRIPTURES

Some do not embrace the need to read or study the Old Testament. They justify this by stating that the Old Testament is the law, and we are under grace; therefore, the Old Testament is nothing more than a historical document. But to fully understand the New Testament, we need to understand the Old. It is important to remember that the Old Testament is the shadow of New Testament truth. If I find a doctrine in the Old Testament, it is a shadow of New Testament truth. If I cannot find a New Testament truth, my understanding of the Old Testament shadow is incorrect. The reverse is also true. If I embrace a New Testament doctrine, I should be able to find the Old Testament shadow. If not, then it is possible that my understanding of the New Testament doctrine is incorrect.

The Old Testament is the start and origin of the recorded words and actions of

Adversity, Trials, and Tribulations

Adonai through the ages of time. There's much wisdom and the history of who we are, and this includes both redeemed and not redeemed. In the Old Testament Scriptures, we see how the Old Testament relates to mankind and his relationship to Adoni in the past, present, and future.

We see the world around us and then can read just how it was wonderfully made! Men wrote the Scriptures in the Old Testament of God, which Adonai also inspired, showing us how important it is to understand what the Lord has done to express His nature and characteristics. His promises and declarations are forever entered when He spoke to his servants. One good example is of the servant was Abraham.

God called Abraham to go! Let me ask a question. Has God called you to do something, and do you know what it is? Have you put the very thing you know to be something He has shown to you to the side, trying to second guess yourself?

Genesis 12: 1 (ESV) Now the LORD said to Abram, "Go from your country and your

Terry L. Scott

> ***kindred and your Father's house to the land that I will show you.***

We can see the first thing that happened was the Lord said to Go. The second was to leave his family behind, trusting the Lord to show him the direction he was to go.

> ***Gen 12:2 (ESV) And I will make of you a great nation, and I will bless you and make your name great, so that you will be a blessing.***

The Lord told Abraham what was going to happen when he obeyed the Lord. He would become a great nation; he (Abraham) would be blessed and be a blessing.

> ***Gen 12: 3 (ESV) I will bless those who bless you, and him who dishonors you I will curse, and in you all the families of the earth shall be blessed."***

Look, now we see even more what the Lord did. He said anyone who blessed Him would be blessed; those who dishonored Abraham would be cursed. All families of the earth would be blessed through him! The most exciting part is all families of the earth shall be

Adversity, Trials, and Tribulations

blessed through him! WOW! That means us today. We are all descendants of Abraham if we have received Yeshua into our lives.

The conversation between God and Abraham explains the Covenant with Abraham so clearly in Genesis 15:1-21. It also laid out Abraham's future in detail and who would be his heir. It was the nation of Israel and the covenant God declared that He would never break.

> *Gen 15: 3 Then Abram said, "Look! You have given me no seed, so a house-born servant is my heir." 4. Then behold, the word of Adonai came to him saying, "This one will not be your heir, but in fact, one who will come from your own body will be your heir." 5. He took him outside and said, "Look up now, at the sky, and count the stars—if you can count them." Then He said to him, "So shall your seed be." 6. Then he believed in Adonai, and He reckoned it to him as righteousness.*

You see God's character throughout the Old Testament concerning His great love for mankind. The Lord was always providing a covenant with man to show him how to live.

Yet man failed God time and time again. The Lord never gave on us. Throughout time, we can see how much He has done for us and how much we have turned away from what He has told us to do to remain in fellowship with Him.

God knew He would have to deal with man in a way only He would understand, so He sent His only son Jesus (Yeshua), born of a virgin. Christ walked on the earth, teaching us how we could walk in His footsteps. Yet the footsteps would be, for the believer committed to a life of walking in faith, truth, and righteousness before the Lord Jesus Christ with a broken and humble Spirit before the Lord.

God provided for Adam and Eve even though they disobeyed Him. He searched for them, He found them, and He spoke to them. Genesis 3:9. God did not send them out naked out of the Garden. He provided them with clothes made of animal skins. God provided all this and reached out to man despite his rebellion against Him. God loves mankind! He does not love the sin of mankind.

Look at the covenant God made with Abraham (the first Hebrew) through

Adversity, Trials, and Tribulations

circumcision. Abraham grew stronger in faith. God told him to offer his son Isaac a burnt offering to prove his faith (Gen 22:1-19). Abraham obeyed and brought Isaac to Mount Moriah and laid him on the altar. The Lord told him not to kill Isaac and gave him a ram for the sacrifice at the last minute. Here we see Abraham's faith (Heb 11:17-19) and a beautiful picture of Christ. The Bible calls Abraham a friend of God: James 2:23, Isaiah 41:8

The way He preserved mankind through Noah, and once again, His covenant with man proved that He would never destroy the earth with water again. We see this description through the rainbow in Genesis 9:13.

The New Covenant, made for all mankind, was shown through the Lord Jesus Christ (Yeshua is Hebrew for Jesus, and the word means salvation!) To fully understand what Jesus did on the cross and why He came to the earth, read the entire chapter of Hebrews 9.

APPLICATION

The Old Testament shadow is the New Testament substance. The Old Testament saints were men and women of deep faith. The Father has called us to a life of faith. Without faith, it is impossible to please God. What are you willing to do today by faith that you would look like a fool if the Father did not show up?

CHAPTER 5

THE OLD TESTAMENT LEVI IS THE NEW TESTAMENT BELIEVER

If we understand the Old Testament and how it connects to the New Testament of the Bible, we can begin to fully understand just how much God has provided for His people. When we read through the Old Testament Exodus, Leviticus, and Numbers, for example, many people will not see the handy work of God. Then in Hebrews 9, we can see how the Scriptures in the old and new are tied together in unity. The whole Bible is like this if we study it, proving that the Word of God is truly unique.

We must pay attention to the whole Bible and not just part of it to begin to fully understand just what the Lord wants to show us through the portals of past, present, and future. A good example is a quick review of the tabernacle to learn more about God and His Character.

OUR GOD IS A GOD OF:

♦ Order:

The details or the tabernacle reveal that God is a God of order. When the Lord brought 2.5 to 3 million Israelites out of Egypt to the desert, He knew that man would need some order to follow God. The way God had the Israelite tribes camp around the tabernacle shows His divine order. The direction of each camp led the tribes in different directions, and this order determined which tribes would go out first.

♦ Holiness:

God, the Creator of the Universe, came down to the earth to reside among sinful man in the tabernacle. God wanted to reveal how evil people could become before the Creator of the universe and attempt to communicate with a Holy God.

The tabernacle showed us the honor and respect we should have before God.

The tabernacle shows the sinfulness of mankind and raises a standard of the esteem we should have before God.

Adversity, Trials, and Tribulations

Details of the Tabernacle reveal the value of the sacrifice Yeshua paid for us on the cross. In the Old Testament, we need to understand that the animal they raised for their living was required to sacrifice to cover their sin at a place before a Holy God. We can miss the value of how important it is to understand the relationship of the sacrificial lamb. We need to see how the comparison of the Old Testament sacrifice foreshadowed the coming of Yeshua the Messiah.

The Lord came down to the earth to reside in a Tabernacle with man. God later sent his Son Jesus (Yeshua) to come to the world and walk and be among man to show us how to walk in God's righteousness. He also came to die for the sins of mankind, showing us we no longer need to go into the tabernacle for the forgiveness of sin. Once and for all, the way was provided for the forgiveness of the sin of mankind through the death, burial, and resurrection of Yeshua the Messiah and not through the blood of bulls and goats as before.

The Lord looked down throughout the pages of time and saw that man would need to be shown how to live in this life. He loved us so much. Yeshua came to die for all mankind.

In Yeshua, there is no time. That is why He can see everything before Him. He is our advocate if we have received Him as the Lord of our lives. Yeshua stands before us and will defend His people.

He is also the soon and very soon returning Lion from the tribe of Judah. You see, He came as a sacrificial lamb to die for the sins of mankind and will return as the Lion from the tribe of Judah, and with a ROAR, HE will return to the earth to take His Throne on the earth as King of Kings and Lord of Lords. We will forever be with Him. AMEN!!!!!!

Mal 3:3 (KJV) And He shall sit as a refiner and purifier of silver and he shall purify the sons of Levi and purge them as gold and silver that they may offer unto the Lord an offering in righteousness.

Mal.3:3 is an Old Testament shadow of the New Testament "royal priesthood."

1 Peter 2:9 (KJV)

Adversity, Trials, and Tribulations

But ye are a chosen generation, a royal priesthood, an holy nation, a peculiar people; that ye should shew forth the praises of him who hath called you out of darkness into his marvelous light:

The New Covenant the Lord made for all mankind was through the Lord Jesus Christ, Yeshua in Hebrew, Jesus in English. The word Yeshua means salvation. To fully understand what Jesus did on the cross and why He came, let's read the entire chapter of Hebrews 9.

God established a plan to allow the Levi priest to go into the Tabernacle of the Lord to offer the people's worship, sacrifice, and prayers. There were guidelines that they had to follow established by the Lord. There were three places in the tabernacle: the porch, the Holy Place, and the Holy of Holies.

In the Old Testament, only the Priest could enter the Holy of Holies. Today the tabernacle is the believing person in Yeshua. We are the believers in Yeshua, covered by His sacrifice thru His Blood on the cross. The Blood of Yeshua.

Heb 9:22 (ESV) Indeed, under the law, almost everything is purified with blood, and without the shedding of blood there is no forgiveness of sins.

If you wanted to know why Jesus died on the cross, this is the reason. In the Old Testament, there could be no forgiveness of sin without sacrificing the blood of bulls and goats. So, we see how Yeshua completed this once and for all on the cross.

Heb 9:24 (ESV) For Christ has entered, not into holy places made with hands, which are copies of the true things, but into heaven itself, now to appear in the presence of God on our behalf.

Yeshua, Jesus is our lawyer defending us as believers and will stand in defense for us when we go before God.

Heb 9:25 (ESV) Nor was it to offer himself repeatedly, as the high priest enters the holy places every year with blood not his own, 26. for then he would have had to suffer repeatedly since the foundation of the world. But as it is, he has appeared once for all at the end of the ages to put away sin by the sacrifice of himself.

Adversity, Trials, and Tribulations

Yeshua came once and died for the sins of all mankind. We do not have to keep going to the tabernacle to make the sacrifices of bulls and goats. It is finished. Praise Adoni!

Heb 9:27 (ESV) And just as it is appointed for man to die once, and after that comes judgment,

Will we live twice and die once? To live twice means to be born of the flesh and the Spirit. When the time comes, we are born twice will die once and be redeemed from the second death.

Or will we live once and die twice? To live once means to be born of the flesh only, and this lack of being born in the Spirit means we will live and die in our sins in this body. Therefore, all who are born once will qualify for the second death after judgment.

Heb 9:28 (ESV) so Christ, having been offered once to bear the sins of many, will appear a second time, not to deal with sin but to save those who are eagerly waiting for him.

We are saved and no longer bound to the things that hold us down! Yeshua (Jesus) did it all. We are no longer bound or held down by the enemy. Jesus told us He would return to save us. AMEN! We must occupy until He comes again. The Book of Hebrews shows us so much about how much God loves us. You see how He reached down to His people by providing a way to communicate directly with Him.

APPLICATION

If you are a true believer, then you are the temple of God because the Holy Spirit has tabernacled within you. You do not belong to yourself anymore, but God has purchased you for His glory. In what ways will you purposely declare today that you are the temple of the Most High God?

CHAPTER 6

HOW ARE GOLD AND SILVER REFINED?

According to Mal.3:3 and other related Scriptures, we know that the believer is refined, as gold and silver. The refining process is to purify the believer. How can we identify the process, and how do we know when it is completed?

Gold has a beautiful yellow color and is rarely in a pure state. In a pure form, gold has three defining characteristics.

- ♦ Refined pure gold is soft
- ♦ Refined pure gold is pliable
- ♦ Purified pure gold is free from corrosion.

Gold is mixed with other metals such as copper, iron, and nickel to make it more rigid and less pliable, thus more corrosive. When combining these substances with gold, the materials are "alloys." The higher the

Adversity, Trials, and Tribulations

percentage of alloy, the more complex the gold becomes and more acceptable to corrosion.

PSA 12:6 (ESV)The words of the LORD are pure words, like silver refined in a furnace on the ground, purified seven times.

Isa 48:10 (ESV) Behold, I have refined you, but not as silver; I have tried you in the furnace of affliction

Rev 3:18 (ESV) I counsel you to buy from me gold refined by fire, so that you may be rich, and white garments so that you may clothe yourself and the shame of your nakedness may not be seen, and salve to anoint your eyes, so that you may see.

APPLICATION

Is it not astonishing to know that we are more significant than gold and silver in the eyes of the Father? Is it somewhat sobering knowing that He refines us like gold and silver to remove the impurities?

Adversity, Trials, and Tribulations

CHAPTER 7

A HEART THAT IS REFINED

Now we see the characteristics of pure gold processed by the Fire. Refined gold is soft, tender, pliable, and noncorrosive. A pure heart before God is like pure gold. A pure heart is soft, tender, and flexible before the Lord and is not corrupted underworldly conditions.

Hebrews 3:7-13 (KJVA)
Wherefore (as the Holy Ghost saith, To day if ye will hear his voice, 8Harden not your hearts, as in the provocation, in the day of temptation in the wilderness: 9When your fathers tempted me, proved me, and saw my works forty years. 10Wherefore I was grieved with that generation, and said, They do always err in their heart; and they have not known my ways. 11So I sware in my wrath, They shall not enter into my rest.) 12Take heed, brethren, lest there be in any of you an evil heart of unbelief, in departing from the living God. 13But exhort one another daily, while it is called

Terry L. Scott

Today; lest any of you be hardened through the deceitfulness of sin.

How do I know I have a refined Heart? I would like to share a short example of a refined heart that the Lord can use. I would like to compare refining silver and how the Lord will refine us to his image.

A man watched how the silversmith held a piece of silver over the fire and let it heat up. To refine the silver, the silversmith needs to hold the silver in the middle of the fire where the flames are the hottest, burning away all the impurities. The man thought about God having him in the center of the flame (trials of this life) of the hot spot; then he remembered Mal.3:3.

Malachi 3:3 (ESV) He will sit as a refiner and purifier of silver, and he will purify the sons of Levi and refine them like gold and silver, and they will bring offerings in righteousness to the LORD.

He asked the silversmith if it was confirmed that He had to sit there in front of the fire the whole time the silver was refined. The silversmith answered yes, He not only had

Adversity, Trials, and Tribulations

to sit there holding the silver, but He had to keep his eyes on the silver the entire time it was in the fire. If the silver stays a moment too long, it flames and is then destroyed. The man thought for a moment in silence. Then asked the silversmith, "How do you know when the silver is fully refined?" The silversmith replied, "when I see my image in it."

In the example, you can see how we, as true believers, will be held to the center of the fire or trials of life and not destroyed because the Lord is watching over us. I noticed that the Lord speaks that His image would not be seen through us if He did not watch over us.

I would like to encourage you not to attempt to escape or bypass the trials but go through whatever fire of life the Father has you in. As you are going through that fire, know that the Lord is right there watching over you.

APPLICATION

The refining process always requires fire. In this case, the Father uses the Holy Spirit to refine us. The Holy Spirit uses adversities, trials, and tribulations in the process. Without the refining process, our hearts will become cold and hardened, and filled with impurities. When the refining process is complete, our hearts are soft and pure. In what areas is God working on you? Are there areas that you have resisted God's refining process, and you have allowed yourself to remain hardened?

CHAPTER 8

A HEART THAT HAS ALLOYS ADDED

We must be careful of allowing sin to remain with our hearts. Sin is the alloy added to a heart that hardens the heart, and this causes a loss of sensitivity. Losing sensitivity hinders our ability to hear the voice of our heavenly Father. The white-hot love and passion for God are replaced with self-love, which seeks pleasure and personal gain.

> *1 Tim. 6:5 (KJVA)*
> *Perverse disputings of men of corrupt minds, and destitute of the truth, supposing that gain is godliness: from such withdraw thyself.*

> *James 1:27 (KJVA)*
> *Pure religion and undefiled before God and the Father is this, To visit the fatherless and widows in their affliction, and to keep himself unspotted from the world.*

APPLICATION

Unconfessed sin, and a refusal to repent or turn from sin, can cause a hardened, calloused, and cold heart. Your assignment is to keep your prayer list for yourself up-to-date. Stay current in confession and repentance.

CHAPTER 9

OUR LORD JESUS CHRIST IS RETURNING FOR BELIEVERS WITH A REFINED HEART

Ephesians 5:27
That he might present it to himself a glorious church, not having spot, or wrinkle, or any such thing; but that it should be holy and without blemish.

Have you ever worked for bosses and liked them because they also knew how you felt? They came up through the ranks, never forgot where they came from and experienced the issues of the everyday work environment. In this same way, we see Jesus as the King of Kings. He is the Creator of all things. God sent his only Son to walk among us, and He set the standard as He grew on the earth to show us we could walk in the Holiness of his Father. Yet, He still experienced the same everyday issues we face today. Let's read the Word in Revelation 12:11.

Revelations 12: 11 (KJVA) And they overcame them by the Blood of the Lamb and the Word of our Testimony, and they loved not their lives unto death."

The temptations of sin are defeated, and the Power of God is displayed through our testimonies. The Word of God will defeat the enemy if we are speaking it in faith and trusting the Lord as we walk with Him every day. A refined heart is a heart created by God and changed and filled with the love of God as we go through the refining process here on the earth while we are alive. We love the Lord even more than our own lives, even unto death.

APPLICATION

Our Lord Jesus Christ will return for a pure, spotless body and not a dilapidated, worn-out old hag. What are you doing to make and maintain yourself in the position of "be ye holy as God is holy?"

CHAPTER 10

REMOVING THE ALLOYS THAT CAUSE CORROSION

One of the characteristics of pure gold is its resistance to rust and corrosion. Changes in the atmosphere with moisture cause rust and corrosion in alloys. The higher the alloy in gold, the more it will tarnish or show decay. The alloy of the world within the Body of Christ has caused the church to tarnish, rust, and corrode away. Values become polluted with worldliness.

> *Malachi 3:3*
> *And he shall sit as a refiner and purifier of silver: and he shall purify the sons of Levi, and purge them as gold and silver, that they may offer unto the Lord an offering in righteousness.*

I walk toward the Lord and not away from Him, no matter what the cost of the call to continue in the work of the Lord, knowing He is the Author and finisher of my faith.

Adversity, Trials, and Tribulations

1 Thessalonians 4:4
That every one of you should know how to possess his vessel in sanctification and honour;

We should continually be walking in a way to glorify the Lord and not the sins of the flesh. We need to walk through what we talk about.

2 Timothy 2:20-21
20. But in a great house there are not only vessels of gold and of silver, but also of wood and of earth; and some to honour, and some to dishonor. 21. If a man therefore purge himself from these, he shall be a vessel unto honour, sanctified, and meet for the master's use, and prepared unto every good work.

To refine gold, the refiner crushes it into powder and mixes it with flux. The two are then placed in a furnace and melted with intense Fire. The alloys or impurities stick to the flux and rise to the top. They are called the dross, which is then removed, thus leaving just the pure gold.

Isaiah 1:25-26

And I will turn my hand upon thee, and purely purge away thy dross, and take away all thy sin: [26] And I will restore thy judges as at the first, and thy counsellors as at the beginning: afterward thou shalt be called, The city of righteousness, the faithful city.

Jerusalem was corrupted, but the Lord said He would deal with the issue and how, He was going to do it. The Lord would and still will purge away the sin or dross by the refining fires of our life. It can be a long-drawn-out process, or it can be short. It depends on how much we let the Lord show us the issues we must go through and our willingness to call out to the Lord.

Proverbs 25:4
Take away the dross from the silver, and there shall come forth a vessel for the finer.

The dross here is talking about moving away, and the result is an improved and purer silver. The dross seen reveals the sin in our lives, and its rising to the top demonstrates our willingness to repent of the sin the Lord shows us through the fire we are going through.

Adversity, Trials, and Tribulations

Ezekiel 22:17-22
And the word of the LORD came unto me, saying, 18. Son of man, the house of Israel is to me become dross: all they are brass, and tin, and iron, and lead, in the midst of the furnace; they are even the dross of silver. 19. Therefore thus saith the Lord GOD; Because ye are all become dross, behold, therefore I will gather you into the midst of Jerusalem. 20. As they gather silver, and brass, and iron, and lead, and tin, into the midst of the furnace, to blow the Fire upon it, to melt it; so will I gather you in mine anger and in my fury, and I will leave you there, and melt you. 21. Yea, I will gather you, and blow upon you in the Fire of my wrath, and ye shall be melted in the midst thereof. 22. As silver is melted in the midst of the furnace, so shall ye be melted in the midst thereof; and ye shall know that I the LORD have poured out my fury upon you.

In Ezekiel 22, we see that many of the sins of Israel are still in America today. We see how in Israel, the wrath of God fell upon the people and how the Lord was purging them and exposing their sin. Now today, we can see how many other countries have followed the same evil way. We can all see how the hand of

God is doing the same thing today as He did in the past. God is exposing the sins of the nations. Many people who once followed the Lord have now turned their backs on the Creator of the universe and now face the same judgment.

They (Israel) made a conspiracy of the prophets by stealing the treasures of the Temple and devouring souls, falsely prophesying.

They (Israel priesthood) had violated the laws of God and profaned the Holy things. They showed no difference between clean and unclean and hid their eyes from sabbaths. The Lord was profaned before them. The princes are like wolves ravening to prey, shed blood, and destroy souls to get dishonest gain.

There was dishonest gain and robbery from the poor and needy. The strangers were included. In Ezekiel 22:31, we see how the Lord had had enough and consumed them all with His fire and wrath. The Scripture comes to memory that the fear of the Lord is the beginning of wisdom. May we all have that fear and walk before the Lord in truth and

Adversity, Trials, and Tribulations

holiness before the King of Kings and Lord of Lords.

APPLICATION

We know the Scriptures say that bad company corrupts good morals. The Scriptures also tell us not to love the world nor the things of the world. Do a self-assessment today and ask the Lord if you are keeping the right company and show you any area where you love the world or the things of the world.

CHAPTER 11

GOD WILL USE HIS FIRE TO REFINE US

Isaiah 48:9-10
For my name's sake will I defer mine anger, and for my praise will I refrain for thee, that I cut thee not off. 10. Behold, I have refined thee, but not with silver; I have chosen thee in the furnace of affliction.

The true believer in the Lord will understand Isaiah 48:9-10. That is because they have been through or going through the refining fire of the Lord. That is why the Lord wants us refined with fire to grow and to walk in the righteousness He has established. In the Old Testament, we can see how the Lord provided a fire to give direction where they needed to walk. The Fire of God not only refines, but it will also direct us where we need to go.

Zechariah 13:9

And I will bring the third part through the Fire, and will refine them as silver is refined, and will try them as gold is tried: they shall call on my name, and I will hear them: I will say, It is my people: and they shall say, The LORD is my God.

The fires of God are needed. The Word describes here something essential. First, we will be refined as a believer. Second, as we are refined, we call on the Lord. Third, the Lord will hear us. Fourth, the Lord acknowledges us as we call out to Him as His people. Fifth, the people of God say the Lord is their God.

Another way to express this is to say because we are believers, we will be refined as silver and gold. This refining is an action we all will go through in life, and we must call on the Lord to help us. The Lord then hears us and answers us. We then declare the Word of the Lord in our lives. The Lord is God.

Malachi 3:2-3
But who may abide the day of his coming? and who shall stand when he appeareth? for he is like a refiner's Fire, and like fullers' soap: 3 And he shall sit as a refiner and purifier of silver: and he shall

Adversity, Trials, and Tribulations

purify the sons of Levi, and purge them as gold and silver, that they may offer unto the LORD an offering in righteousness.

The Lord is raising His people, both Jew, and Gentiles, to be one in the Messiah and one in the Olive tree. He is purifying us with the trials of life that come our way. I will stand on only one thing in this life, and that is what the Word of Yeshua has told me to do.

1 Peter 1:6-7
Wherein ye greatly rejoice, though now for a season, if need be, ye are in heaviness through manifold temptations: 7That the trial of your faith, being much more precious than of gold that perisheth, though it be tried with Fire, might be found unto praise and honour and glory at the appearing of Jesus Christ:

The trial of our faith and how we respond are very, very important. I choose to continue through this trial, knowing that the Lord is praised and always honored through it.

APPLICATION

Us having adversities and going through trials and tribulations is a given fact. However, if we do not embrace them and allow them to do their work in refining us, all we get out of the process is damaged and frustrated. How we handle the fire of the Holy Spirit is the key to maturing in our Lord. Self-assessment time again. Have you tried to embrace the work of God's refining fire, or have you tried to escape it because you have been taught to avoid anything uncomfortable?

CHAPTER 12

GOD USES ADVERSITY, TRIALS, AND TRIBULATIONS AS A MEANS OF HIS REFINING FIRE.

How has the Lord used trials and tribulations to shape you into the believer you are today? Most believers have gone to the woodshed for a good correction. The next set of Scriptures express this very well and give us hope to know that the Lord has not forsaken us when we are going through these challenging and difficult times in our lives.

Hebrews 12:5-11
And ye have forgotten the exhortation which speaketh unto you as unto children, My son, despise not thou the chastening of the Lord, nor faint when thou art rebuked of him: 6. For whom the Lord loveth he chasteneth, and scourgeth every son whom he receiveth. 7. If ye endure chastening, God dealeth with you as with sons; for what son is he whom the father chasteneth

not? 8. But if ye be without chastisement, whereof all are partakers, then are ye bastards, and not sons. 9. Furthermore we have had fathers of our flesh which corrected us, and we gave them reverence: shall we not much rather be in subjection unto the Father of spirits, and live? 10. For they verily for a few days chastened us after their own pleasure; but he for our profit, that we might be partakers of his holiness. 11. Now no chastening for the present seemeth to be joyous, but grievous: nevertheless, afterward it yielded the peaceable fruit of righteousness unto them which are exercised thereby.

James 1:2-4
My brethren, count it all joy when ye fall into divers temptations; 3. Knowing this, that the trying of your faith worketh patience. 4. But let patience have her perfect work, that ye may be perfect and entire, wanting nothing.

We see that the fire applied to gold removes the alloys that make it hard and corrosive. Gold refined, becoming pure, soft, and pliable, without spot or corruption. Fasting is critical in this process. The Spirit is willing, but the flesh is weak. The Lord Jesus

Adversity, Trials, and Tribulations

Christ told the disciples right before critical times of testing to pray and fast.

> **Matthew 26:41**
> **Watch and pray, that ye enter not into temptation: the Spirit indeed is willing, but the flesh is weak.**

We often wonder what it is like to pray and touch the heart of God. You can see the perfect example when Jesus prayed in the Garden of Gethsemane. He knew that the people were coming to take Him to His death on a cruel cross. The feelings Jesus must have experienced knowing He was about to suffer on the cross.

> **Matthew 26:39**
> **Again, for the second time, he went away and prayed, "My Father, if this cannot pass unless I drink it, your will be done."**

Jesus asked His Father to take this away from Him, and He asked the Father if there was another way. You can see just how much pain the words of a loving Savior spoke, and yet He knew He had come to die for all of mankind. He said the words, which set into action the Hand of God that would change the fate of mankind from death to life. Our Lord was obedient to suffering and death.

> ***Philippians 2:8 And being found in appearance as a man, He humbled Himself by becoming obedient to the point of death: death on a cross.***

I am so very grateful for what Yeshua did on the cross for me. We can never thank Him enough for the sacrifice He made for mankind on that day He died for crimes He did not commit. One of the most common statements concerning this is that Jesus paid a debt He did not owe because we owed a debt we could not pay.

> ***Matthew 26:44 So, leaving them again, he went away and prayed for the third time, saying the same words again.***

Jesus spoke this prayer to his Father three times. During the prayers at Gethsemane, the disciples did not understand what would happen at that moment. Only Jesus did because He was filled with the Holy Spirit and praying to His Father. Our Lord knew the pain and torment He must go through for our redemption. You can see just how much the

Adversity, Trials, and Tribulations

disciples did not understand that He was about to be crucified on a Roman cross.

Jesus even told them two times to stay awake, and at the third time, He warned them in Matthew 26:45-46.

> **Matthew 26:45-46 Then he came to the disciples and said to them, "Sleep and take your rest later on. See, the hour is at hand, and the Son of Man is betrayed into the hands of sinners.46. Rise, let us be going; see, my betrayer is at hand."**

How often has the Lord Jesus Christ called us to be prayer warriors and watchmen on the wall? We see how much spiritual warfare is taking place, and many of us are spiritually asleep. Have we grown tired as the Church that we cannot pray when the Lord wakes us up in the middle of the night to pray and intercede for a specific situation? I am guilty of this before and was shown just how vital prayer was to the Lord through the Scripture. I was just like the disciples at Gethsemane. He showed us how we must always pray in good times and turmoil. We are in the last days when the return of the Lord Jesus Christ, the King of Kings, is coming!

While reading this, the Lord has been calling you to pray or move forward in the Lord. I only can say what Jesus said to the disciples. WAKE UP and do what the Holy Spirit is telling you to do. Pray, seek to understand, and know the will of God for your life. Move forward in the calling He has set before you. Complete what the Lord has called you to do before you die. Jesus never expected us to do anything He did not do. He did everything out of love, and we are to do the same. The refining fire of God will cleanse us as we walk and mature in Him every day, walking in a humble and brokenness the Lord Jesus Christ told us to follow.

Adversity, Trials, and Tribulations

APPLICATION

Our Lord Jesus Christ set the example for us in everything and every area. We may be quick to quote John 14:12 in that we can do the works of Jesus and greater works than what He did because He went to the Father. However, one of the works of our Lord was to suffer for righteousness' sake. He gave us an example and taught us how to take up our cross and die daily. What areas do you need to die to today?

CHAPTER 13

THE WILDERNESS EXPERIENCE

Along with the trials and tribulations, the Father uses to refine us, and there is also the "Wilderness Experience." It always seems that when I am in the Refiners fire that I find myself in the wilderness. There are three essential questions I would like to answer.

- What is the "Wilderness Experience?
- Why do we go through the Wilderness?
- Why does the "Wilderness Experience" seem to happen when I need God the most

Even Job understood the frustration of seeking God so hard in so many places and ways only not to find Him. Sometimes when I fast or pray more earnestly or read and study the Word more intensely, things that are not so pleasant just "happen," and God seems a million miles away. Let us read what Job was doing as God seemed to be playing hide and seek with him.

> ***Job 23:8-9***
> ***Behold, I go forward, but he is not there; and backward, but I cannot perceive him: 9.On the left hand, where he doth work, but I cannot behold him: he hideth himself on the right hand, that I cannot see him:***

Have we not all been there with Job? Seeking God in what seemed to be our darkest hour, and it looks like God is nowhere. We know from the Word of God that He is present and that He loves us, but His manifest presence seems to be absent. It seems at times that all we get is silence when seeking God with all our hearts and in need of a comforting Word from our Father. So, the "Wilderness Experience" is when God pulls back His manifested presence and seems to be far from our lives. The fire experience is when God is refining an area in our hearts.

During these desert times, we pray, and our minds go back to another time when we say, "there was a day when all I had to do was whisper God's Name and His manifested presence was immediately there." But now, in the stillness, emptiness, and silence, we want to shout, "*God, where are you?*"

In the "Wilderness Experience," I rest in the knowledge that we are not alone. We are walking where Moses, Abraham, David, and Job walked, used mightily by God. The wilderness is a necessary time, a season of life for all of God's children. Of course, we wish that it could be bypassed in our flesh and that we can get to maturity without it. That is the microwave mentality that many of us have adopted over the years of modern conveniences. We want patience, and we want in now! It is in our nature to look for a shortcut to get all that God has for us.

The road to heaven is achieved by going through the wilderness first. Remember that the "promised land," which was flowing with milk and honey, had giants and famines also. We feel as though our flesh and soul have dried up and flaked away in the wilderness times. In the wilderness, we long to see God move in our lives and the lives of those around us. We once again desire to see God move in His power and grace. We learn to appreciate the things we have in God the Father,

Adversity, Trials, and Tribulations

especially His anointed presence. King David expressed all of this in Ps.63.

> *Psalms 63:1-2*
> *A Psalm of David when he was in the wilderness of Judah. O God, thou art my God; early will I seek thee: my soul thirsteth for thee, my flesh longeth for thee in a dry and thirsty land, where no water is; 2. To see thy power and thy glory, so as I have seen thee in the sanctuary.*

APPLICATION

There are plenty of "fair-weather" Christians in the world. The fair-weather believers are those who can only rejoice and praise God when things are going well in their lives. Job had lost everything, yet he said, "though God slays me, I will praise Him." The question Satan asked God is this, "Does Job love You for nothing?" In other words, Christian, do you need everything to be perfect before you can praise and love God, or can God remove everything you love, and will you still worship Him? OUCH!

CHAPTER 14

THE WILDERNESS EXPERIENCE WOULD SEEM AS THOUGH GOD HAS FORSAKEN US

In Psalms 22:1-2, we find the words of King David, which our Lord Jesus Christ uttered as He hung on the cross. Both in the message of David and that of our Lord, we see that they cried out that in their darkest hours of tribulations and trials, the Father seemed to withdraw His manifested presence and placed them in a "Wilderness Experience."

Psalms 22:1-2
To the chief Musician upon Aijeleth Shahar, A Psalm of David. My God, my God, why hast thou forsaken me? why art thou so far from helping me, and from the words of my roaring? 2. O my God, I cry in the daytime, but thou hearest not; and in the night season, and am not silent.

APPLICATION

As kids, many of us loved the game hide and seek. As parents or grandparents, we still play hide and seek with our children and grandchildren because they love it. It does my heart well when I see the delight in their eyes when they search and find me. Sometimes I hid hard to make them search with all their heart. So it is with the Father. Although He never leaves us, He will pull back His manifested presence, and we may feel that God moved a thousand miles away. He wants to seek Him with all that is in us. What will you do today to seek the Father with all your heart?

Adversity, Trials, and Tribulations

CHAPTER 15

THE WILDERNESS EXPERIENCE MAY SPARK THE QUESTION, "WHERE IS YOUR GOD?"

In Ps.42, we see the fire in trials and tribulations simultaneously of the wilderness experience. It was a time when the emotions were down, almost depressed, yet through obedience, the sons of Korah continued to praise God. In the "Wilderness Experience," we learn to anchor our souls on the Rock of our Lord. Then no matter what comes our way or how fearful the enemy may seem, we remain steadfast and grounded and able to praise the King of Glory.

Psalms 42:1-11
To the chief Musician, Maschil, for the sons of Korah. As the hart panteth after the water brooks, so panteth my soul after thee, O God. 2. My soul thirsteth for God, for the living God: when shall I come and appear before God? 3. My tears have been

my meat day and night, while they continually say unto me, Where is thy God? 4. When I remember these things, I pour out my soul in me: for I had gone with the multitude, I went with them to the house of God, with the voice of joy and praise, with a multitude that kept holyday. 5. Why art thou cast down, O my soul? and why art thou disquieted in me? hope thou in God: for I shall yet praise him for the help of his countenance. 6. O my God, my soul is cast down within me: therefore will I remember thee from the land of Jordan, and of the Hermonites, from the hill Mizar. 7. Deep calleth unto deep at the noise of thy waterspouts: all thy waves and thy billows are gone over me. 8. Yet the LORD will command his lovingkindness in the daytime, and in the night his song shall be with me, and my prayer unto the God of my life. 9. I will say unto God my rock, Why hast thou forgotten me? why go I mourning because of the oppression of the enemy? 10. As with a sword in my bones, mine enemies reproach me; while they say daily unto me, Where is thy God? 11. Why art thou cast down, O my soul? and why art thou disquieted within me? hope thou in God: for I shall yet praise him, who is the health of my countenance, and my God.

Adversity, Trials, and Tribulations

Psalms 10:1
Why standest thou afar off, O LORD? why hidest thou thyself in times of trouble?

APPLICATION

In the Song of Solomon, when the Shulamite woman went out seeking the King, the women of the city asked her, "What is so special about your lover that you seek him so hard?" Sometimes when we are under the fire of adversities, trials, and tribulations, the world may ask us, "Where is your God now?" We need to rejoice in the good times and the difficult times and Paul and Silas in prison. What testimony are you leaving among lost people when you have difficult times? Do they walk away asking, "Where is your God now?"

CHAPTER 16

UNDERSTANDING THE TIMES THAT WE ARE IN

1 Chron. 12:32
And of the children of Issachar, which were men that had understanding of the times, to know what Israel ought to do; the heads of them were two hundred; and all their brethren were at their commandment.

We are living in incredible days. There are wars and rumors of wars. The economic crisis has seemed to have reached a global proportion resulting in financial ruin for millions. As we understand the times, we will understand the Biblical course of action as to what we ought to do. We must know what it is the Father wants us to accomplish. In the "Wilderness Experience," as we are experiencing the fire of God, we need to discern what the Father is doing in and through us. Otherwise, we find ourselves reacting to the symptoms we are experiencing instead of the root issue.

One example recorded in the Word of God concerning this would be the story of the lame man at the Temple gate in Acts 3:1-10. He had been lame from birth and was carried to the Temple gates each day to beg for money. Here is a man who had not discerned the times he was living. The Lord Jesus Christ had walked among them and now had ascended into the heavens. Jesus had commissioned and empowered His disciples to do the work of the ministry. Peter and John had come to the Temple to pray and saw the lame man, who begged them for money. Because the lame man had not discerned the times in which he lived and those who walked among him, he had asked Peter only for what he needed to satisfy his need for the day. He had lost sight of his actual condition, the fact that he could not walk. Peter brought the lame man back into the reality of his real need, the need to stand and walk and be healed.

> *Acts 3:1-8*
> *Now Peter and John went up together into the Temple at the hour of prayer, being the ninth hour. 2. And a certain man lame from his mother's womb was carried, whom they laid daily at the gate of the*

Adversity, Trials, and Tribulations

Temple, which is called Beautiful, to ask alms of them that entered into the Temple; 3. Who seeing Peter and John about to go into the Temple asked an alms. 4. And Peter, fastening his eyes upon him with John, said, Look on us. 5. And he gave heed unto them, expecting to receive something of them. 6. Then Peter said, silver and gold have I none; but such as I have give I thee: In the name of Jesus Christ of Nazareth rise up and walk. 7. And he took him by the right hand and lifted him up: and immediately his feet and ankle bones received strength. 8. And he leaping up stood, and walked, and entered with them into the Temple, walking, and leaping, and praising God.

APPLICATION

Time for self-assessment. Have you prayed and sought to be out of your current situation, or are you praying and asking God what needs to be changed in your heart while in your current situation? Do you want God to heal the result of the heart condition or the root and cause of the heart condition?

CHAPTER 17

GOD DESIRES TO REVEAL WHAT HE IS DOING AND WHY HE IS DOING WHAT HE IS DOING

I know this is a radical statement and cannot hang there by itself, but God desires to show us His plans and His ways. He does so in believers who have a heart of righteousness and desire to serve and love Him.

> *Genesis 18:17-18*
> *And the LORD said, Shall I hide from Abraham that thing which I do; 18. Seeing that Abraham shall surely become a great and mighty nation, and all the nations of the earth shall be blessed in him?*

> *Psalms 25:14*
> *The secret of the LORD is with them that fear him; and he will shew them his covenant.*

> *Hosea 14:9*

Who is wise, and he shall understand these things? prudent, and he shall know them? for the ways of the LORD are right, and the just shall walk in them: but the transgressors shall fall therein.

Amos 3:7
Surely the Lord GOD will do nothing, but he revealeth his secret unto his servants the prophets.

Luke 12:54-56
And he said also to the people, when ye see a cloud rise out of the west, straightway ye say, There cometh a shower; and so it is. 55. And when ye see the south wind blow, ye say, there will be heat; and it cometh to pass. 56. Ye hypocrites, ye can discern the face of the sky and of the earth; but how is it that ye do not discern this time?

Sowing a seed is essential, but equally important is sowing it in good soil and at the right time. One would not plant a tomato plant in the rocks in the winter months. It is terrible soil, and the time is not correct, so the seed is lost. The farmer needs to understand these three things.

- ♦ The Seed

Adversity, Trials, and Tribulations

- The Soil
- The Season.

To understand God's pruning time with us, we must recognize God's season in our lives.

> **John 15:2**
> **Every branch in me that beareth not fruit he taketh away: and every branch that beareth fruit, he purgeth it, that it may bring forth more fruit.**

The Greek word "purge" is "kathairo" and means to *cleanse*, to *prune*. God uses the fire by way of trials and tribulations and the wilderness to do this.

> **2 Timothy 2:21**
> **If a man therefore purge himself from these, he shall be a vessel unto honour, sanctified, and meet for the master's use, and prepared unto every good work.**

> **Eccles. 3:1**
> **To every thing there is a season, and a time to every purpose under the heaven:**

- There is a plowing season
- There is a sowing season

- There is a watering season
- There is a weeding or pruning season
- There is a harvest season
- Then there is the WILDERNESS season

THE WILDERNESS SEASON

The wilderness season is preparing the ground of our hearts for another time. The foundation gives nothing back at the moment.

So, the wilderness is not a negative time for those who obey the Lord. It is a time to prepare and train for the next move of the Holy Spirit in our midst. There are many ways to respond to the wilderness time that the Lord has us in. How do you react to your wilderness season?

NOTE: We enter the wilderness mostly without knowing it is coming and often react to it without wisdom.

Adversity, Trials, and Tribulations

APPLICATION

The heavenly Father loves us who believe as His children. Since we are His children, He does not wish to work in a vacuum keeping us in the dark. God tells us to consider our ways and to consider the times. Ask the Father which season of your Christian life are you in currently. Is it time for plowing, sowing, watering, weeding, or harvest?

Terry L. Scott

CHAPTER 18

TYPICAL RESPONSES FROM BELIEVERS TO TRIALS, TRIBULATIONS, AND THE WILDERNESS TIMES

PRAYER TO ESCAPE THE DISCOMFORT

When the wilderness times come, our typical natural response is to assume that it is an attack from the enemy, so we seek out a prayer ministry time. Getting prayer from one another should be an encouragement. Problems occur in life. We must not see every trial and tribulation as an attack from the enemy. We should discern and embrace the fact that the Father may be addressing issues of the heart. We, as believers, have been taught that all discomfort is from the enemy. Believing that every trial and tribulation is an attack from the enemy is not found in the Word of God.

Adversity, Trials, and Tribulations

Another response to trials and tribulations is that we typically start looking for what is wrong within us. We ask ourselves, "have I sinned" or "is there something wrong in the church or with the leadership"?

Or we start looking for an escape route, like faster music, more Bible reading, or more time in prayer.

Another approach is to allow the enemy to use the wilderness time to beat ourselves up, and then we find ourselves walking around in depression.

Another approach to dealing with wilderness time is to smile and pretend that all is okay. With this, we could be hurting emotionally, mentally, spiritually, or physically and when asked, we tend to answer, "I'm fine."

These reactions to the wilderness only cause the prolonging of the wilderness time because God is committed to working out His purposes in and through us. If not careful in discerning the time we are in our reaction process will lead us to frustration, hardheartedness, and a sense of loneliness and defeat. Israel's lack of understanding of their wilderness time caused an entire generation to die in the wilderness and forced them to lose their destiny. See the Exodus story. Because they viewed Egypt as a better place than the wilderness, they could not understand that God was working out His plan and destiny. This attitude caused them to rebel and murmur against God and His leadership. So, what does this story have to do with us? I had heard Christians comment that they were better off before they were saved.

> *1Co 10:1-12*
> *Moreover, brethren, I would not that ye should be ignorant, how that all our fathers were under the cloud, and all passed through the sea; 2. And were all baptized unto Moses in the cloud and in the sea; 3. And did all eat the same spiritual meat; 4. And did all drink the same spiritual drink: for they drank of that spiritual Rock that followed them: and that Rock was Christ. 5. But with many of them God was not well pleased: for they were overthrown in the wilderness. 6. Now these things were our examples, to the intent we should not lust after evil things, as they also lusted. 7. Neither be ye*

Adversity, Trials, and Tribulations

idolaters, as were some of them; as it is written, The people sat down to eat and drink, and rose up to play. 8. Neither let us commit fornication, as some of them committed, and fell in one day three and twenty thousand. 9. Neither let us tempt Christ, as some of them also tempted, and were destroyed of serpents. 10. Neither murmur ye, as some of them also murmured, and were destroyed of the destroyer. 11. Now all these things happened unto them for ensamples: and they are written for our admonition, upon whom the ends of the world are come. (12) Wherefore let him that thinketh he standeth take heed lest he fall.

Their ignorance of God's ways caused them to react in wickedness, but those who understood the ways of God and the timing of the wilderness experienced His will and the promised land.

APPLICATION

We live in a society where many are always looking for a loophole or an escape clause. We all are going to go through adversities, trials, and tribulations. We might as well forget any thoughts of finding spiritual, mental, emotional, or physical loopholes or escape clauses. Ask the Lord to make you ready to embrace His refining fire daily.

CHAPTER 19

WHY DO WE GO THROUGH THE TOUGH TIMES?

Many times, I get asked the question of why so many bad things happen to good people. Because of the things that I see in the body of Christ, I see more clearly why the Holy Spirit was leading me to prepare this book. Believers as a whole feel as though the enemy has placed them in a cooking pot, and God does not care. I am here to say that trials are a good thing because they originate with the Father.

Trials are to correct us, purify us, reveal issues of the heart hidden so that we can repent of them, and release the character of God within us. Trials in themselves cannot produce these things. How we react, or should I say if we are PROACTIVE to them, is what creates the character of God in us. Read Matt. 5 and 6 and see how we should act under trials and tribulations. See also 1 Thess. 5, Rom. 5, and Jam. 1. These chapters give us the Biblical responses that God wants when things are not so pleasant.

Trials do not necessarily mean that we are in sin as an individual, as a family, or as a church. But we grow through trials. You can teach your children proper behavior week after week. You will not know if you got through to them, nor will they have a chance to incorporate that teaching unless a trial comes where they need to make a choice.

Now sickness is not a trial all the time. There are many reasons someone gets sick, which we will cover later. Sickness, disease, or retardation can result in a person's test but from a different viewpoint.

Trials and tribulations are not temptations. Temptations are from the heart of man. Temptation is the lust that is within our hearts. The enemy can only successfully tempt us in the lust areas of our hearts. Attractions can become trials because if we give in to the temptation, we find ourselves in consequences that could be trials. Example: Suppose my funds are low and I don't have extra to spend anywhere. Now I am driving through town in

Adversity, Trials, and Tribulations

a 30mph speed zone at 60mph. The police pulled me over and gave me a costly ticket, and removed my driving license. Now the temptation was to drive faster than the posted speed. The trial and tribulation came when the consequences of giving in to the temptation caused a more significant financial problem because of the speeding fine and difficultly due to losing my license.

I have had people say that the trials in their lives have caused great turmoil, and my response to this is WHY? Problems do not cause disruption, but our reaction to them does. In the Book of Acts, we do not find Paul asking God why he was stoned and left for dead twice, shipwrecked, beaten, imprisoned, snakebite, and many other things. He is the one who wrote that these are opportunities to praise the Father.

The Lord is teaching us that we as a Church, we as families, and we individually cannot come to the place to praise and honor the Lord and maintain the faith when all in well in the camp. Will we praise when all is not well? Will we praise in the abundance of trials? When it rains, it pours.

Trials come in groups, but we have the promise from the Father that He knows our limit and our "breaking" point and will not allow us to be tried, tested, or tempted beyond that point. I have often stood up in the middle of a trial or temptation and said, remember to praise God, I am still standing, and I am still in the faith. Having the belief to remain is what Jesus prayed for Peter. Jesus prayed Peter would still be found in the faith at the end of the trial. So have faith that God is taking care of you realize that part of the taking care is developing His character within you. There is also the process of reaping what you sow, living in unconfessed sin, rebellious heart, and other such things that I am not covering now. I am dealing only with those who are walking with the Lord and are undergoing trials. Now, I left open many other questions, such as the many reasons sickness comes on someone. It helps us know how to pray.

Why do we go through hard times? You ask yourself. Many people do not understand why I'm going through this difficult trial, and I'm a believer. What should I do? Well, the Lord Jesus Christ is testing. We decide what

Adversity, Trials, and Tribulations

we are made of, and if they're not made of the right material, He's refining us into gold and silver in the refiner's fire, whether we like it or not. Those that are obedient to the fire will fall on their knees in brokenness and humbleness and call upon the name of the Lord Jesus Christ. He is the Alpha and Omega, the beginning and the end.

So, we can see how one example of a patriarch in the Old Testament went through many trials and tribulations without even really understanding why. Job had faith in God. Job knew God was in control, and his faith alone sustained him through the test of the Lord. God even told Satan when Satan came up before God's in the throne room, "look at Job, the Lord said. He is blameless." My servant is blameless. Do you know what blameless means? It means we're walking perfectly before God. Now you must remember that Jesus had not yet come, and this was before the tabernacles and before the Torah was brought forth to instruct Israel on how they should go.

I recommend you read the story of Job in the Bible. Take each chapter one at a time and pray about it. Understand that it's about all of us, not just a story in the Old Testament. You will see many of your lives, my life, and what's happening around you or the world. When you read the Book of Job, it's good to remind yourself what Job said, summarizing the whole book about him, what he went through. Job said, The Lord giveth, and the Lord take it away. Bless it, be the name of the Lord.

Those are powerful words from a man beaten down by the trials and tribulations of his life. Job lost his family, everything he had, and everything he owned because the devil thought he could take away his faith in God. Satan thought he could remove Job's protection and destroy him.

I pray that we will intently look at our lives and see just how well God has protected us through our trials and tribulations. We have the power and authority in our Lord Jesus Christ to handle trials and tribulations as Job did. I pray we will take the time to seek the Lord in our quiet time away from all distractions and things that would separate us from God's voice. First, we need to hear Him

Adversity, Trials, and Tribulations

concerning our salvation by receiving His Holy Spirit in our lives. As we walk in the newness of life our Lord gives, we begin to understand when He speaks and His will for our lives.

We can see perseverance in the faith by Job in the Old Testament before the Torah was even present in Israel. Job walked blamelessly before the Lord, and he was a type or shadow of our Lord Jesus Christ. We can see how Jesus came and walked blamelessly in this world, showing us how we can live victorious Christian lives if we follow Job's example in how he dealt with things.

Job had three friends, and when they approached him, they all tried to help him, telling him he should repent before the Lord. The friends of Job were convinced that he must have done something wrong. Yet, Job said that he had done nothing wrong. Job was assured that he was okay with God because he had just talked to Him and asked why he was suffering. The third person that spoke to Job said to him, "Why is this happening?" He tried to reason with Job that he needed to repent of his sin. Job's friend reassured Job that he would be forgiven and healed. But Job replied, "No. I've done nothing wrong." Job then told his friends to leave, and he spoke to God directly. The next time Job spoke, he talked to God directly, and that's when God said to him in a way that Job was deeply humbled, and he fell on his face.

And that's when he spoke in his final words, saying. The Lord giveth. The Lord takes away. Bless it, be the name of the Lord. We should always have this in our hearts no matter where we go, what we're doing, or what the circumstances are. Remembering Job's words will help get us through this world we live in today. Many people forget that we need to walk in brokenness and holiness before the Lord, knowing that He is the author and finisher of our faith. God will guide us through this world no matter what we're going through and keep us strong. The Father will teach us to do battle to and fight against the tricks, trials, and adversities that come our way in everyday life?

You can see the mediation going on between Job and the Lord. The Lord was talking to Job while Job meditated on what was being done to himself. He attempted to explain

Adversity, Trials, and Tribulations

all the circumstances he had gone through. God was refuting them while showing Job who He was and how Job forgot why He was there until the holiness of God fell on Job. When the presence of the Lord fell on Job, he finally answered back to Him in humbleness.

How many times in our life does God reach us and speak to us and tell us that we should come to Him in holiness and humbleness before his throne. We must remember that He is the author and finisher of our faith and that He has called us to be faithful even in an unfaithful world. But notice one thing I thought of before I was writing this. How the adversary wants to bring us down, make us believe we're nothing, and try to distract us and make us think we are way off track. We are on track, probably more on track than we ever were. We don't see it because we're distracted by the things that the adversary has thrown in our paths. Let us all fall on the knees and pray before the Lord most high and give Him the glory He rightly deserves. Remember that it is the Lord who gives, and it is the Lord who takes it away. May He always bless you and keep you, and may He shine His light upon you. I bless you with the shalom upon your life. Forever and ever and ever, Amen.

Adversity, Trials, and Tribulations

APPLICATION

Lord, I know that I must go through these times for my good so that You will be glorified. Teach me to be faithful as I embrace Your work of refining me for Your honor.

CHAPTER 20

THE TRIALS OF MY LIFE

I wanted to show in this chapter the trials of my life and how I have come through them. As I write them, I pray that they will speak to others to see some similarities they have gone through or may be going through now to help and encourage.

What do you think is the best way to share who Jesus is? You may answer, "with His Word, through the testimony of our Christian walk and how we came to receive the King of Kings in our hearts.

I grew up in a family of seven in Enterprise, Alabama. I was the youngest of two older brothers and sisters. My dad was a soldier in the US Army, and my mother stayed home and helped raise us while my dad was always away fighting wars until he retired and came home after the Korean and Vietnam wars. My mother would help keep us in clothes and food because my dad did not make

Adversity, Trials, and Tribulations

enough money for all the children then. My mom probably worked harder than my dad ever realized back then, taking care of each of us alone.

Dad served in the Korean war and two extensive tours in Vietnam during the height of the most brutal fighting. We would watch the news and see the daily casualties on TV, not knowing if my dad was one of them. Even as a child back then, I saw how it caused me to want to be just like my dad. I wanted to be a soldier because that was all I saw around me growing up.

Dad was one of the blessed few who survived the Vietnam and Korean Wars and came home alive. The Lord allowed me to honor my father in his later years by being there for him after my brother, sister, and mom died from cancer within a year apart. It seemed we were going to funerals each year and wondered who was going to be next. I worked as a government employee and served overseas. I regularly had to fly home for another funeral. I learned to hate those long flights. Then my Father died at age 89 after seeing mom and his two other children die.

I was back in the US and retired to help him go through some arduous dark hours of his life. We would talk about the Lord and what he had been through, along with what was ahead. He knew he was going to die. I asked the Lord to use me again as a vessel to honor and bless my earthly dad while he was alive and make sure he would be with Jesus when he died.

I experienced something like what Job went through when he lost all his family as I witnessed my family members die one by one. One of the best things that happened to me was reaching out to my dad and sharing the love of Jesus to him on his death bed in a veteran's home in Mobile, Alabama, just before he passed away. My dad served in many combats and had a Silver Star, and the scars of the heart most true war veterans do not share. I can understand this because I, too, was in a war. The 17-hour drives from Culpeper, VA to Mobile, Alabama and Enterprise Alabama wore me out, but I would not give up. It was because I loved and respected my dad and wanted to be with him, and I knew he would go to be with the Lord soon.

Adversity, Trials, and Tribulations

I can understand the love Jesus had for His Father and the respect that He would be obedient to Him and die for the sins of all mankind. I did not worship my dad, but I did and still do honor his memories. It reminds me of who Jesus is and what exactly He did for me, a sinner who is saved by Jesus' death on the cross. I can do nothing but fall on my face and give Honor to the King of Kings and Lord of Lords.

I had to decide to either let the circumstances beat me up and destroy my life or allow the events to strengthen who I am in the Lord Jesus Christ. I chose to allow them to make me stronger to battle the enemy as I had to deal with many other issues during this time.

I grew up most of my life what most would call army brat and knew what a PX (Post Exchange) or BX (Base Exchange) was. We later moved off the base, Ft. Rucker, Alabama, when my dad purchased a home in Enterprise, Alabama, right outside of Ft. Rucker.

I attended the local school systems and graduated in 1978. During the years of school, I was always into sports. I ran track, played football and basketball depending on the season of the sport. I had to ride a bicycle 10 miles every day to school because I wanted to be involved in the sports program, and my mom could not take me from school because of the size of our family. She had to cook and feed all of us. Why did I want to play sports? It was something I had to do. It later allowed me to be one of the fastest runners in the area and prepare for entry into the military right after graduation.

The adversity I encountered early on in my life started with the issues of my heart. The Lord revealed to me what they were, and as I saw myself as someone who truly needed to repent and come to the Lord Jesus Christ at Abbot Loop Christian Center while I was in the Air Force on active duty at Elmendorf AFB, Anchorage, Alaska.

I will never forget the day I was born again. It was a life-changing experience for me. I heard the evangelist Dick Irwin preaching. The Holy Spirit, along with, I believe, a few

Adversity, Trials, and Tribulations

angles, helped me to go forward at the altar. I walked, which turned to a run as I approached the altar, where Dick Irwin led me to the Lord that day. I was baptized in water in the name of the Lord Jesus Christ. I will never forget that day I went down in the water and came up. I could sense a white robe put on me. I knew the Lord had sealed me until the day He calls me home or the day He will return. That is when my journey to serve the Lord began.

I often wonder what has changed in the church. Why do the people never go down to the altars for repentance or prayer anymore? Jesus did say in:

> *Matthew 10:32(ESV) So everyone who acknowledges me before men, I also will acknowledge before my Father who is in heaven, 33. but whoever denies me before men, I also will deny before my Father who is in heaven.*

We are told we had to acknowledge Jesus before man for Jesus to be our advocate in the presence of God.

> *Luke 12:8(ESV) I tell you, everyone who confesses Me before men, the Son of Man*

will also confess him before the angels of God.

Jesus is our advocate.

Luke 15:10(ESV) In the same way, I tell you, there is joy in the presence of God's angels over one sinner who repents."

The angels of God rejoice over one sinner coming to Jesus.

Romans 10:9(ESV) that if you confess with your mouth, "Jesus is Lord," and believe in your heart that God raised Him from the dead, you will be saved.

The change comes from the heart.

Psalms 119:46 (ESV) I will speak of thy testimonies also before kings and will not be ashamed.

Jesus is our advocate. We will be given the words to speak before the people He sends us to share the Gospel of the Lord Jesus Christ.

Let's go out and share the Love of the Lord Jesus Christ to all who will hear. I was

Adversity, Trials, and Tribulations

radically saved but also radically changed. The things I once did, I did not want to do them anymore.

Once I came to the Lord, there have been many adversities in my life. The enemy is out to destroy the true believer in any way he can, but by the grace of God, I am standing alive today. The Lord showed me a long time ago when I came to him that I would serve him and go wherever He sent me. Little did I know He would send me to the nations. All along, the Holy Spirit dealt with the matters of my heart and areas I needed to overcome. He is still doing that today and making me what I was created to do and be (like Jesus).

We will all go through adversity in our lives. Look at them as ways the Lord Jesus Christ can shape us in His image. Adversity helps us change those areas that need to be changed and make us a beacon of the truth of the Lord. Our victories through the hardships of life are like sounding the Shofar of the Lord to a lost and dying world before Yeshua returns.

Well, let's speed forward through my life to the year 2016. I had to be medevacked back from overseas due to a brain tumor. I was experiencing the most severe pain in my head and right eye you would ever know. I wanted to die because the pain was so bad. It felt like a thousand pin needles stabbing me in the back of my head and my eye.

First, I had been rushed to a foreign doctor, where they found the brain tumor on my brain stem. It was the size of a lemon and pressing on other parts of my brain. This tumor was very deep, and they could do nothing to help me except medicate me for the flight home. I was sent back to the US to a hospital called Inova Cancer Center. There the doctors completed many tests on me, such as MRI's and blood work.

The Doctors treated with one dose of radiation using a medical procedure called cyberknife. It was a non-invasive way to reach the brain stem without having to do the surgery using radiation. I had to follow up with a three-month MRI to see the brain tumor had changed or shrunk.

Adversity, Trials, and Tribulations

Once I returned to the US, I continued having constant struggles with headaches and being tired all the time. I had decided to retire from the federal government and deal with the issue in prayer with my wife. We both prayed and believed the Lord would heal me.

The first six months, it did shrink down from the size of a lemon to a pea. I was so happy and went back to work in 2017. I still had to have follow-up MRIs and take medication. We did not know what type of tumor this was still but could only treat it and hope and pray for the Lord to destroy it.

I started to have headaches and took different medications. An MRI showed the tumor had grown and needed to be removed before it grew to size to cause issues with my brain and my whole body.

In an appointment with the Neurosurgeon on February 8, 2021, I elected to have brain surgery right away to try and remove the mass on my brain stem. The neurosurgeon set up a team to perform the craniometry on the right side of my head for March 15, 2021.

Let me pause here and say something. This brain issue was adversity that could have killed me. I was asking the Lord so many questions, and then the Lord spoke to me these words. DO YOU LOVE ME? I was so focused on my issues and pain I forgot to trust the Lord. I felt like this was an issue going on too long. The truth of the matter was the Lord needed to make significant changes to my heart condition to allow me to remember who I was in Christ and be obedient to what He set before me, even if it meant physically dying! Yes, I said physically dying.

The Lord was not just testing me but was showing me the condition of my heart. I had areas in my heart of doubt. You remember, I saw my mom, brother, and sister die of cancer. This illness made me face the fears of dying, along with realizing there was a generational curse over my family, which was trying to take out the whole family any way it could.

During this time, I prayed along with my wife that whatever we must go through, we trusted the Lord to be with us and provide

Adversity, Trials, and Tribulations

a way as He did for the children of Israel. We are holding on to the Word of God and nothing else. I have learned to cast down every vain imagination that exalts itself above the Word of God.

The most challenging time through all this was having to say goodbye to my wife and not knowing that I would live or die during the surgery to extract this brain tumor off my brain stem. We kissed and prayed. In the surgical preop, I called the surgical team and prayed the Lord would be with them all to do their jobs and the Lord would guide the hands of the surgeon. During the seven-and-a-half-hour surgery, at some point, I felt as if I was awake and could see a large man leaning against the wall of the operating room next to a large oxygen cylinder, with his arms crossed and staring at me. He had a beard with curly brown hair. When I looked at him, He spoke to me without talking and said everything would be ok. Then I fell back to sleep.

When I was being moved to ICU after the surgery, I had a stroke in my brain and had to be treated right away. Once they stabilized me, they evaluated me to see what or if there was any damage done. So, through the surgery, the stroke, and the recovery, we saw the hand of God all around, protecting me to live and not die.

The surgery only removed a section of the tumor to see what type it was through a biopsy. I am told the tumor has been gowning again since the surgery on March 15, 2021. Since then, I have not been able to work anymore and have exhausted my financial resources through investments to pay bills. I did go through re-habilitation and was able to learn to talk, eat, and walk. I still have issues but only know what the Lord spoke to me in the operating room, "everything was going to be ok."

I must throw in a little story here to make you smile. The people in the church had to hire a new pastor, and there were two choices. One was a young man fresh out of Bible school, and the other a much older man with a walking stick. He was not as handsome, but you could see the scars from living a rough life before. The final decision came, and the church was together and decided to choose the older man.

Adversity, Trials, and Tribulations

When the young man found out he was not selected, he was angry. He asked why they chose the older man. The church said they did not want someone full of theology and pride. They needed someone to help guide them through the trials and storms of life. The church wanted someone who would be on his knees in prayer and fasting. They finally stated they knew the older man was the right choice because they would never select someone who did not walk with a limp.

On a computer or sheet of paper, I encourage you to write down your testimony and share it with those around you. Maybe your life adversities have left you with a limp. It might be physical, emotional, mental, relational, or financial, but you know what it is like to face adversity, wrestle with your faith in God, and still stand with a strong testimony.

APPLICATION

Lord, we all have a testimony of going through the hard times, but we don't all have a testimony that honors You. May I be found faithful no matter what comes my way! In my life or my death Lord, I ask that You be honored and that I leave a Godly testimony.

CONCLUSION

The Holy Spirit has taught me to walk each day, one day at a time. Doing so has helped me see the physical issues around my life and understand daily spiritual ones. Each day my life of faith will determine how I will fight them and discern what the Lord is showing me?

I pray the Lord will guide, encourage, and direct you through all the storms and adversities of your lives. Your adversities are nothing compared to what the Lord Jesus Christ did for you. He was born through a virgin, walked, lived as a man, and He was the Son of God in the flesh.

Jesus showed us how we could walk and have eternal life through Him, taking all the suffering and pain for humanity upon Himself on the cross. He suffered, died, buried, and rose from the grave, conquering death, hell, sin, and the grave! Jesus' self-less action allowed all people the opportunity to come to him and repent from the heart. This act of faith will allow Him to change us and give us a new start, walking in a humble, obedient heart before the King of Kings.

ABOUT THE AUTHOR

Terry L. Scott came to the Lord on November 27, 1989, at Abbott Loop Christian Center while stationed in the USAF at Anchorage, Alaska. The Lord has opened many doors for Terry to serve Him and be a part of unique ministry opportunities in America, Europe, Africa, Asia, and the Middle East. Terry and his wife Ana currently reside in Culpeper, Virginia, serving the Lord.

Made in the USA
Middletown, DE
02 December 2021